"YOU HAVE MADE US FOR YOURSELF, AND OUR HEARTS ARE RESTLESS UNTIL THEY FIND THEIR **REST** IN YOU."

Augustine, *Confessions 1.1*

A RULE OF LIFE

FOR REDEMPTIVE ENTREPRENEURS

TABLE OF CONTENTS

Preamble 4

How to Consider This Rule 8

The Rule in One Page 10

Time 14

Money 18

Imagination 22

Decision-Making 26

Power 30

Community 34

THIS IS A RULE OF LIFE FOR ENTREPRENEURS AND OTHERS CALLED TO ENTERPRISING LEADERSHIP.

OUR MOST SIGNIFICANT **IDENTITY** IS NOT AS ENTREPRENEURS OR LEADERS.

We are citizens in God's kingdom and members of God's household, and we are members of earthly families and households, part of neighborhoods, communities, and nations. The way of faithfulness for us is not fundamentally different than it is for any person: seeking to love God and our neighbor with our whole heart, soul, mind, and strength, by repenting and believing the good news.

At the same time, the gifts and traits that draw us toward entrepreneurship, and the social context that surrounds us as entrepreneurs, pose particular temptations. They also offer us unusual and visible opportunities to live joyfully distinct lives of faith, hope, and love.

The use of a rule of life — a set of practices to guard our habits and guide our lives — goes at least back to the Old Testament figure Daniel. As an exile, Daniel was in an unfamiliar cultural context that provided no support for the practice of his faith — and as a leadership trainee in the court of Babylon, he was exposed to powerful pressures for assimilation to Babylon's dominant ethos. He and his companions committed themselves to a vegetarian diet instead of "the king's rations" (Dan. 1) and developed the practice of praising and praying to God three times a day in front of an open window (Dan. 6:10).

Similarly, at many times in history, notably in the monastic movements, Christians with particular vocations have adopted a particular rule. At its best, a rule of life is an expression of community, undertaken in the belief that we need help from one another to live the lives God meant for us. It also expresses humility, recognizing that we are prone to specific pitfalls that require us to take extra care with our practices.

From the "outside," a rule of life can look limiting. But it is more like musical, athletic, or military training: a set of disciplines that, carried out as "a long obedience in the same direction," give us creative capacities and a creative community that we would not have on our own.

This rule of life is not meant to replace the ordinary practices of faithfulness to which all members of the church are called. But it is meant to guard us and our households from the greatest dangers of our particular calling, and to maximize our opportunity for redemptive influence.

HELP US, GOD,
TO LIVE IN THE
ABUNDANCE FOR
WHICH YOU MADE
US, AND TO BRING
THAT ABUNDANCE
TO EVERY PART OF
YOUR WORLD.

HOW TO CONSIDER THIS RULE

1

Read it as an invitation. When we receive an invitation, we consider the person inviting us, the event or occasion to which we are invited, our own desires, and our ability to say yes or no in our current circumstances.

When you consider the Praxis community, the specific postures and practices of this rule, your own needs for encouragement, growth, and discipline, and the current circumstances of your life, is this an invitation to which God wants you to say yes?

2

Read it with your most important partners. Share it with your closest circle of accountability and discipleship, and with members of your household who would be involved in keeping this rule with you. If you are married, share it with your spouse. Consider discussing it with your pastor, counselor, or spiritual director. Consider sharing it with your business partners.

3

Consider adopting the baseline practices on a prototype basis for four weeks. At the end of that period, consider whether you would like to make them an ongoing part of your discipleship and leadership, along with an intent to explore the reach practices and seek creative approaches in each area.

4

Decide whether to say yes to the invitation. If you decide to say no, consider whether there are alternative commitments you believe God is calling you to make.

5

If you decide to say yes, we invite you to commit to practice this Rule of Life, in dialogue with at least one other person—and to review your progress on a quarterly basis.

A commitment to this Rule of Life is an intention to observe the baseline practices (while also exploring the reach practices and creative approaches), submitting ourselves to trusted others who will remind us of God's grace when we fall short and who will lovingly exhort us to continue growing in these commitments.

THE RULE IN ONE PAGE

TIME

Instead of endless productivity, we practice a rhythm of work and rest, attending to our need to grow in all the dimensions of being human: heart, soul, mind, and strength. We commit to take one full day every week for complete rest from our daily work, and to make Sabbath possible for everyone within our sphere of authority.

MONEY

Instead of being preoccupied with money and possessions, we practice simplicity and generosity. We commit to give away a minimum of 10% of our gross income, with special attention to the needs of the materially poor.

IMAGINATION

Instead of having our imagination saturated by media, we seek to be transformed by the renewing of our mind. We commit to establish structured limits for our use of screens and our consumption of entertainment, in quantity, frequency, and moral character.

DECISION-MAKING

Instead of willful autonomy in decision making, we practice active dependence on God. We commit to daily prayer, and at times of major decisions, making every effort not to proceed until we have actively submitted our own desires about the decision fully to the will of God.

POWER

Instead of accumulating power to benefit ourselves or exploit others, we use it to generate possibility for those who have less access to opportunity. We commit to the practice of gleaning—frequently sacrificing opportunities for our own advancement to intentionally create pathways for others. We also practice chastity and fidelity, honoring the men and women with whom we work.

COMMUNITY

Instead of individualism and isolation, we practice real presence with others who are not part of our daily work. We pursue diversity across class and ethnicity in our friendships and mentoring relationships.

OUR PRACTICES WITH

MONEY

TIME

IMAGINATION

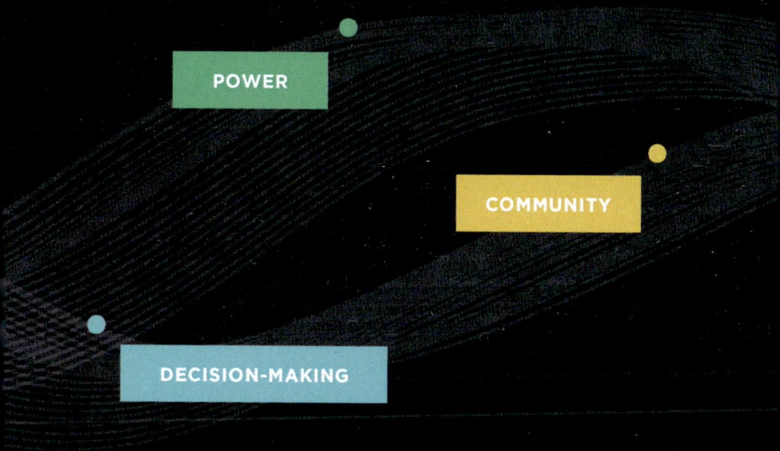
POWER
COMMUNITY
DECISION-MAKING

TIME

OUR REALITY

Our vocation tends to make us both eager to work hard and constantly haunted by a sense of urgency and busyness. It also often deprives us of opportunities to balance mental and emotional effort with the development of our soul and our physical body.

INSTEAD OF ENDLESS PRODUCTIVITY, WE PRACTICE A RHYTHM OF **WORK AND REST,** ATTENDING TO OUR NEED TO GROW IN ALL THE DIMENSIONS OF BEING HUMAN: HEART, SOUL, MIND, AND STRENGTH.

BASELINE PRACTICE

As a baseline, we commit to take one full day every week for complete rest from our daily work, and to make Sabbath possible for everyone within our sphere of authority. Those of us in roles that almost exclusively emphasize mental activity also commit to regular physical exercise that develops our strength and endurance.

REACH PRACTICES

As reach practices, many of us aspire to:

1. Follow Daniel's example of stopping for prayer three times a day—at the beginning, middle, and end of day.

2. Plan for sabbaticals — extended periods of rest, recreation, and reflection — for ourselves and members of our team.

CREATIVE APPROACHES

We seek creative approaches that include finding new ways to incorporate rest and physical health into the lives of work teams and their families, recognizing that without our active endorsement, they may feel direct or indirect pressure to constantly produce and perform.

HOPE FOR ABUNDANCE

We hope for abundance in the form of joy at work well done, a diminished sense of hurry and anxiety, embodied enjoyment of creation, and delight at God's provision for us while we rest.

MONEY

OUR REALITY

Our vocation can create significant wealth when we work in the for-profit sector, and often requires significant financial sacrifice when we work in the nonprofit sector. Whatever our compensation, we are wealthy when compared with the rest of the world, and embedded in global systems of materialism and consumerism. And our calling requires careful attention to cash and capital flows.

INSTEAD OF BEING PREOCCUPIED WITH MONEY AND POSSESSIONS, WE PRACTICE SIMPLICITY AND **GENEROSITY.**

BASELINE PRACTICE

As a baseline, we commit to give away a minimum of 10% of our gross income, with special attention to the needs of the materially poor.

REACH PRACTICES

As reach practices, many of us aspire to:

1. Increase both the percentage and absolute amount of our giving over time.

2. Tithe on our assets, not just our income, on a regular basis and at key moments where generosity and dependence on God is most needed.

3. Regularly pray for God to protect us and our organizations from wealth and financial windfalls until we are prepared to be good stewards.

CREATIVE APPROACHES

We seek creative approaches to generosity within the enterprise, since we often have influence or control over the salaries of others, their equity ownership, and more. We seek generous business models that can be implemented throughout the supply chain, from vendors to customers.

HOPE FOR ABUNDANCE

We hope for abundance in the form of freedom from worry about money and preoccupation with possessions, joyful relationships with those we are able to financially support, and true prosperity in the form of healthier families, communities, and nations.

IMAGINATION

OUR REALITY

Our vocation involves extensive use of technology for productivity and promotion, and we are often tempted to relieve stress with entertainment. Over time these patterns entrench a cycle of boredom and distraction, diminishing our ability to cultivate a redemptive imagination.

INSTEAD OF HAVING OUR IMAGINATION SATURATED BY MEDIA, WE SEEK TO BE **TRANSFORMED** BY THE RENEWING OF OUR MIND.

BASELINE PRACTICE

As a baseline, we commit to establish structured limits for our use of screens and our consumption of entertainment, in quantity, frequency, and moral character.

REACH PRACTICES

As reach practices, many of us aspire to:

1. Read Scripture at the beginning and end of the day.

2. Immerse ourselves regularly in creation, where we can experience ourselves as small amidst God's handiwork rather than self-important in our own work.

3. Regular reading of books, both fiction and nonfiction, from all eras of history, in place of electronic media.

4. Disengage from screens of all kinds on a daily, weekly, and annual basis.

CREATIVE APPROACHES

We seek creative approaches to renewing our imagination, such as contemplative prayer, in-depth engagement with Scripture through techniques like lectio divina, encounters with the arts, or in-depth study of particular industries or issues in ways that help us activate our creative imagination for future action.

HOPE FOR ABUNDANCE

We hope for abundance in the form of deeper capacity for concentration and creativity, genuine rest rather than restless leisure, and more effective work and leadership.

DECISION-MAKING

OUR REALITY

Our vocation places us in positions where we are expected and empowered to make major decisions that affect many people.

INSTEAD OF WILLFUL AUTONOMY IN DECISION-MAKING, WE PRACTICE **ACTIVE DEPENDENCE** ON GOD.

BASELINE PRACTICE

As a baseline, we commit to daily prayer, and at times of major decisions, making every effort not to proceed until we have actively submitted our own desires about the decision fully to the will of God.

REACH PRACTICES

As reach practices, many of us aspire to:

1. Fasting (abstaining from food, with modifications as appropriate given individual physical limitations, for at least one mealtime) as a regular discipline, and especially at times when we need discernment and guidance.

2. An ongoing relationship with a spiritual director or pastor who helps us consistently discern how God is working in our life.

CREATIVE APPROACHES

We seek creative approaches
to removing obstacles
to God's will in our life,
such as extended times of
solitude that could expose
the counterfeit gods in our
life, and developing forms of
examen specifically designed
to assist us in saying yes and
no to apparent opportunities.

HOPE FOR ABUNDANCE

We hope for abundance
thanks to the supernatural
provision that comes from
obeying God rather than
merely human insight, and
peace and contentment
at times of both apparent
success and apparent failure.

POWER

OUR REALITY

Our vocation places us in intense working environments that grant us power and status, tempting us to use these gifts for our own control, gratification, fame, and ego—often at the expense or exclusion of others. Our inherited patterns of historical injustice have not afforded equitable shares of power or status to women, people of color, and many others within our vocational reach.

INSTEAD OF ACCUMULATING POWER TO BENEFIT OURSELVES OR EXPLOIT OTHERS, WE USE IT TO GENERATE POSSIBILITY FOR THOSE WHO HAVE LESS ACCESS TO **OPPORTUNITY.**

BASELINE PRACTICE

As a baseline, we commit to the practice of gleaning — frequently sacrificing opportunities for our own advancement to intentionally create pathways for others. We also practice chastity and fidelity, honoring the men and women with whom we work and avoiding the exploitation of our power to attain unearned intimacy.

REACH PRACTICES

As reach practices, many of us aspire to:

1. Actively recruit, develop, and be mentored by women, people of color, and others who have been excluded by histories of systemic prejudice.

2. Implement systems of relentless accountability and transparency for our conduct and relationships, in proportion to our personal influence and celebrity.

3. Devote a significant amount of our charitable giving and investing to ventures led by women and members of historically excluded communities.

CREATIVE APPROACHES

We seek creative approaches to using organizations and institutions to restructure access to opportunity and capital among communities where these have been restricted, through long-term partnerships and networks that rebuild empathy and equity.

HOPE FOR ABUNDANCE

We hope for abundance as God's image bearers — male and female, from all ethnicities and backgrounds — collaborate in all our diversity to a blessed alliance that brings the full range of human gifts to our work.

COMMUNITY

OUR REALITY

Our vocation can easily consume all our time and relational energy, giving us the illusion that our identity comes entirely from our work.

INSTEAD OF INDIVIDUALISM AND ISOLATION, WE PRACTICE REAL **PRESENCE WITH OTHERS** WHO ARE NOT PART OF OUR DAILY WORK.

BASELINE PRACTICE

As a baseline, we commit to regular participation in a worshipping community; including another person (our spouse, if we are married) in evaluating and adjusting our time commitments on a regular basis, especially travel that takes us away from home; and pursuing diversity across ethnicity and class in our friendships and mentoring relationships.

REACH PRACTICES

As reach practices, many of us aspire to:

1. Ongoing accountability groups with friends who have no stake in the outcome of our work, who can hear the full stories of our lives and speak God's truth into our stories.

2. Committing to a consistent, ordinary opportunity to serve others that does not accrue any status or significance for ourselves.

3. Consistently have people from a different socioeconomic, ethnic, or cultural background among our ten most recent phone or messaging contacts.

CREATIVE APPROACHES

We seek creative approaches to being deeply known, such as carefully tracking our time with our family and closest friends, or creating a personal advisory board; to creating ways for our coworkers and members of our households to encounter one another as whole persons; and to reducing the conflict between paid work and our responsibilities to children, aging parents, and others dependent on our care.

HOPE FOR ABUNDANCE

We hope for abundance in the form of being deeply known for who we are rather than only what we do, redemptive encounters with people very different from us, and relationships that are lifelong and extend blessing even beyond our own lives.

Made in the USA
Middletown, DE
07 April 2025

73777063R00024